LET THE GAMES BEGIN!

Maya Ajmera　　　　with a foreword by Bill Bradley　　　　**Michael J. Regan**

SHAKTI for Children

Charlesbridge

The game that is called soccer in the United States is called football in other countries. Captions for pictures of this sport include both names, with the American name listed first. The game Americans call football is played almost exclusively in the United States.

Foreword

On any given day, millions of kids around the globe are playing sports. Why? First and foremost, to have fun. Sports are about having a good time. They are also about life. Sports help young people develop and teach them important lessons:

- To finish a game, especially when you are tired, you must persevere.

- To overcome an injury and get back into the game, you need courage.

- To believe you can win a close game, you need to have confidence in yourself and your teammates.

- To be part of a successful team, you must understand and practice teamwork.

Sports were an important part of my childhood. At an early age, I began playing baseball, basketball, and whatever else was in season. My love of sports led me to a successful basketball career, an Olympic gold medal, and many valuable friendships. The lessons I learned from sports have served me well throughout my life, both on and off the court.

Let the Games Begin! captures the joy of sports and shares so many reasons for getting involved. No matter where you live or what your level of skill or experience, sports can play an important role in your life. I hope this book will be an inspiration to you.

Bill Bradley
U.S. Senate, 1979–1997
New York Knicks, 1967–1977

Basketball in Turkey and Ecuador. Soccer in Guatemala

Wherever you live, you can enjoy sports. You might like making a basket, scoring a goal, running a race, or hitting a bull's-eye. There are lots of choices.

Basketball   Ecuador

Soccer/Football   Guatemala

Swimming in Benin and Mexico. Tennis in Ukraine

and Zimbabwe. Cricket in India and the United Kingdom.

Kids all over the world like sports for the fun, for the friendship, and for the challenge. No matter what sport you play, something exciting and wonderful can happen at any moment.

Track and Field   United States

Archery   Bhutan

and the United States. Skiing in China and Finland.

Sports give you a chance to dream. Imagine being as great as your favorite athlete. You can see yourself hitting a home run, skating the perfect program, or making the winning shot. When you dream, anything seems possible!

Soccer/Football

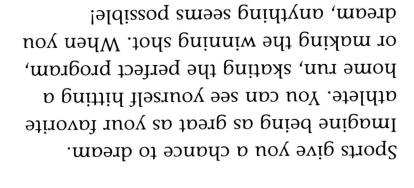

Thailand

Volleyball

Baseball

United States

Israel

Ice-Skating   Russia

Golf   United States

Reach for your dreams by setting goals. Choosing the right goals—ones that aren't too easy or too hard—helps you get to the next level. You might be into sports just for fun, or you might hope to win a championship. Either way, you learn and improve each time you play.

> *"The best way to get started is to play with your friends"*
> —Fei, China

Most kids get started in sports by playing with their friends. After school, it's fun to go swimming or shoot hoops. There are lots of ways to get involved. Try a team sport like softball, cricket, ice hockey, or volleyball. Or choose a sport you can do on your own, like golf, skiing, horseback riding, or gymnastics.

Golf

Kung Fu   China

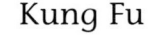

Swimming   Mexico

Play different sports to learn which ones you like most. Your friends, family, and coaches can give you advice. But nobody can tell you what it really feels like to swing a golf club or serve a badminton birdie. To learn a sport, you have to jump into the action.

India

Baseball

United States

Skiing

Finland

Running, jumping, kicking, and flying through the air—in sports you use your body in lots of different ways. You leap, bend, and turn during a gymnastics routine. You wind up to pitch a baseball, crouch as you approach a ski jump, and charge down the field after a soccer ball. Just by playing, you build strength, speed, balance, and coordination.

Gymnastics

Ice-Skating

United States

In-Line Skating   Australia